IMPORTANT JOBS
AT HOSPITALS

by Mari Bolte

PEBBLE
a capstone imprint

Published by Pebble Explore, an imprint of Capstone
1710 Roe Crest Drive, North Mankato, Minnesota 56003
capstonepub.com

Library of Congress Cataloging-in-Publication Data is available on the Library of Congress website.

ISBN 9780756572327 (hardcover)
ISBN 9780756572273 (paperback)
ISBN 9780756572280 (ebook PDF)

Summary: Gives readers basic info about often and less often-considered jobs at hospitals.

Image Credits
Getty Images: bluecinema, 7, ER Productions Limited, 12, FatCamera, 15, Jasmin Merdan, 17, JohnnyGreig, 28, TommL, 8; Shutterstock: CandyBox Images, 19, Frame Stock Footage, 27, Gorodenkoff, Cover (top), Monkey Business Images, Cover (bottom), 5, 25, New Africa, 20, Tyler Olson, 11, YAKOBCHUK VIACHESLAV, 23

Editorial Credits
Editor: Mandy R. Robbins; Designer: Dina Her; Media Researcher: Jo Miller; Production Specialist: Tori Abraham

All internet sites appearing in back matter were available and accurate when this book was sent to press.

Printed and bound in China.   PO5132

TABLE OF CONTENTS

Words in **bold** are in the glossary.

HOSPITALS TO THE RESCUE

No one wants to be seriously sick or hurt. Hospitals can help! People go there for treatment to feel better. But hospitals don't run themselves. Many people work there.

Find out who helps care for **patients** and run a hospital. There is a job at the hospital for everyone. Each one is important!

DOCTORS

Doctors are the first people you might think of when it comes to hospitals. Doctors talk to patients. They find out a person's **symptoms**. Then they make a plan to help the person. Patients come back for check-ups. The doctors see if the symptoms have changed.

There are different types of doctors. Some treat head **injuries**. Others look at skin problems or sew up cuts. Some doctors work only with children.

Doctors go to school for a long time.
There is a lot to learn!

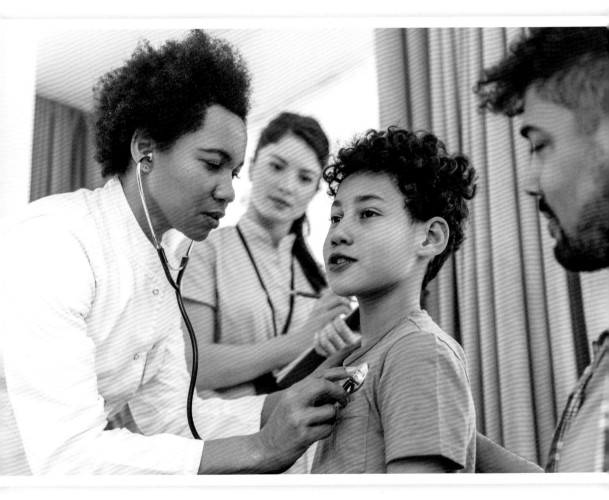

SCHEDULERS

You can't see a doctor without a scheduler. Many people come to the hospital. They plan their visits ahead of time. A scheduler knows when doctors will have time to see a patient.

Schedulers also remind patients when they need to come back. They can pass along a patient's questions to doctors. They can also leave the doctor a note about a person's special needs. Sometimes, visits need to be canceled. Schedulers take care of those too.

XRAY TECHS

Not all injuries are on the outside. An **Xray** machine takes a peek inside someone's body. Some machines are small. They are hand-held! Others are huge. Patients go inside them.

Xray techs know how to use these machines. They take care of them. Then the machines run well.

Patients must be still while Xrays are taken. Techs make sure the patients feel safe. Once the Xrays are taken, the techs look at the image. They help doctors decide if something is wrong.

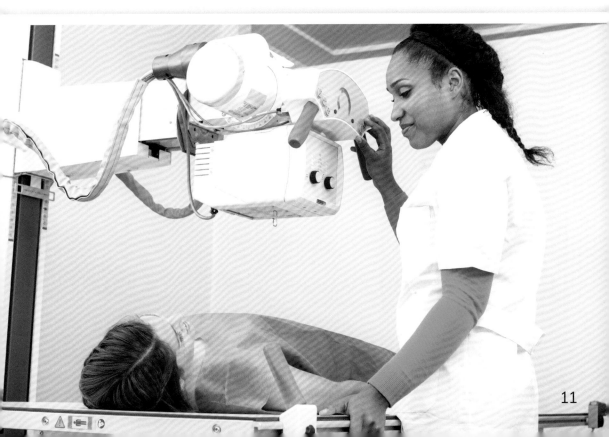

NURSES

Nurses have many jobs at the hospital. They give medicine. They change **bandages**. They keep **wounds** clean.

Most importantly, nurses care for people. They keep patients comfortable. They also talk to patients' families. Having a loved one's health in danger is difficult.

Some nurses actually are doctors. Regular doctors are Doctors of Medicine (MDs). But nurses can also be doctors! A nurse can earn a Doctor of Nursing Practice (DNP) **degree**. MDs learn about medicine and sickness. DNPs learn about caring for patients.

FACT

Many hospitals have phone numbers you can call to speak to a nurse. They can help over the phone or tell you to come into the hospital.

CAFETERIA WORKERS

Everyone at the hospital needs to eat. Patients need food. Visitors might not want to leave to get a meal. Doctors, nurses, and other hospital workers can eat at the cafeteria too.

Cafeteria workers make hot food for lunch and dinner. They sell snacks too. Some people have special **diets**. Others might have **allergies**. Workers make sure meals are healthy and safe. They even deliver the food to patients.

AMBULANCE CREWS

Emergencies can happen everywhere. **Ambulances** rush to the scene of a fire or car accident. They come if someone has a health emergency too.

Workers called EMTs and paramedics are inside. They aren't doctors or nurses. But they can give emergency care to people who need it. They might need to help someone breathe or get warm. They might help someone who is having a heart attack or is choking. They bring sick and injured people to the hospital.

FACT

Ambulances have flashing lights and sirens they can use in an emergency. That way drivers know to get out of the way.

COUNSELORS

Some injuries can't be seen at all. People go through scary or painful events. They might not know how to deal with what happened. Counselors are there to support them. They listen. They talk about what happened.

Helping the person's mind heal is a counselor's job. Trying a new medicine is one idea. Talking to people in a group is another. Knowing other people have gone through the same thing can help.

PHYSICAL THERAPISTS

After being sick or hurt, your body might not work like it did before. Physical therapists help patients get strong again. They make sure the patient does not get too tired. It is easy to overdo it.

Swimming and **yoga** are gentle ways to move. Physical therapists also teach stretches and exercises. Later, patients can do these things at home to keep healing. With a physical therapist's help, patients can heal and have less pain.

VOLUNTEERS

Volunteers help out at the hospital. They may do laundry or clean rooms. Sometimes they read stories or entertain patients. Some give out blankets or treats. Others make hot meals for families who must stay for a long time. Children in hospitals might miss school. Volunteers can help them with homework.

> **FACT**
>
> Animals can volunteer too! Dogs, cats, guinea pigs, and even miniature horses can be therapy animals. Special trainers teach them how to behave in hospitals.

INFORMATION TECHNOLOGY

Computers are very important in hospitals. Patient information is stored there. Schedules, test results, and doctors' notes are all kept online. Patients send their doctors questions through computers. They pay their bills that way too.

> **FACT**
> IT staff make virtual visits possible. Patients can video chat with doctors and nurses.

All that information needs to stay private. Information technology (IT) staff help computer systems run smoothly. They make sure everything stored on computers is safe.

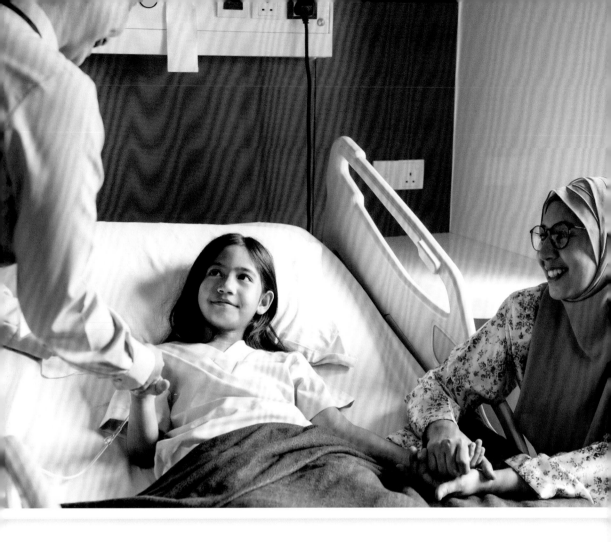

At some point, most people will need
to go to the hospital. Many people
work there to help patients. Every job is
important. Would you ever want to work
at a hospital? What job would you do?

OTHER JOBS AT THE HOSPITAL

Billers

Staying in a hospital can be expensive. Billers figure out how much a hospital stay costs. They send patients and insurance companies a list of costs they need to pay.

Housekeeping

Hospitals create a lot of laundry! Housekeeping makes sure doctors and nurses have fresh and clean sheets, towels, robes, and anything else they might need.

Lab Techs

Doctors might order tests for patients. Lab techs check blood, urine, skin, or other test samples to see if patients are healthy.

GLOSSARY

allergy (A-luhr-jee)—an extremely high sensitivity to something, such as dust, pollen, perfume, certain foods, or animals

ambulance (AM-byuh-luhnts)—a vehicle that takes sick or injured people to a hospital

bandage (BAN-duhj)—a covering that protects wounds

degree (di-GREE)—a title given for finishing a course of study in college

diet (DY-uht)—the kind and amount of food given to a person for a special reason

injury (IN-juh-ree)—damage to a part of the body

patient (PAY-shunt)—a person who gets medical care

symptom (SIMP-tuhm)—a sign that suggests a person is sick or has a health problem

wound (WOOND)—a cut or other injury

Xray (EKS-ray)—a photograph of the inside of a person's body

yoga (YO-guh)—poses and breathing exercises used to improve physical and emotional well-being

READ MORE

Gee, Hey. *My Life Beyond Vaccines and My Community: A Mayo Clinic Patient Story*. Rochester, MN: Mayo Clinic Press, 2022.

Murray, Julie. *Nurses*. Minneapolis: Abdo Kids Junior, an imprint of Abdo Kids, 2021.

Nwora, Christie. *The Hospital: The Inside Story*. New York: Neon Squid US, 2022.

INTERNET SITES

Easy Science for Kids: How to Become a Nurse
easyscienceforkids.com/nurse/

Hospital Facts Revealed for Kids: Know How Hospitals Work!
kidadl.com/fun-facts/hospital-facts-revealed-for-kids-know-how-hospitals-work

The Children's Hospital Volunteers
volunteeratchildrens.org/

INDEX

ABOUT THE AUTHOR

Mari Bolte is an author and editor of children's books on all sorts of subjects, from graphic novels about science to art projects to hands-on history. She lives in southern Minnesota in the middle of a forest full of animals.